KU-132-458

Sizes

Big and Small

Diane Nieker

www.raintreepublishers.co.uk
Visit our website to find out more information about **Raintree** books.

To order:
☎ Phone 44 (0) 1865 888112
▤ Send a fax to 44 (0) 1865 314091
▣ Visit the Raintree Bookshop at **www.raintreepublishers.co.uk** to browse our catalogue and order online.

First published in Great Britain by Raintree,
Halley Court, Jordan Hill, Oxford OX2 8EJ,
part of Harcourt Education.
Raintree is a registered trademark of Harcourt
Education Ltd.

Editorial: Sarah Shannon and Louise Galpine
Design: Jo Hinton-Malivoire
Picture Research: Natalie Gray and
Ginny Stroud-Lewis
Production: Chloe Bloom
Originated by Dot Gradations UK
Printed and bound in China by South China
Printing Company

ISBN 1844 43786 8
10 09 08 07 06
10 9 8 7 6 5 4 3 2 1

British Library Cataloguing in Publication Data
Nieker, Diane
Big and Small – (Sizes)

530.8'1

A full catalogue record for this book is available
from the British Library.

Acknowledgements
Getty Images/DK Images p. **11**; Getty
Images/Stone pp. **8**, **9**, **10**; Harcourt
Education/Tudor Photography pp. **4**, **5**, **6**, **7**, **12**,
13, **14**, **15**, **16**, **17**, **18** (l and r), **19**.

Cover photograph reproduced with permission
of Getty/Imagebank.

Every effort has been made to contact copyright
holders of any material reproduced in this book.
Any omissions will be rectified in subsequent
printings if notice is given to the publishers.

The paper used to print this book comes from
sustainable resources.

Disclaimer
All the Internet addresses (URLs) given in this
book were valid at the time of going to press.
However, due to the dynamic nature of the
Internet, some addresses may have changed, or
sites may have changed or ceased to exist since
publication. While the author and publishers
regret any inconvenience this may cause readers,
no responsibility for any such changes can be
accepted by either the author or the publishers.

Some words are shown in bold, **like this**. They are explained in the glossary on page 23.

Contents

What does small mean?

Small things take up less space.

Look at these boxes.

The pink box is small.

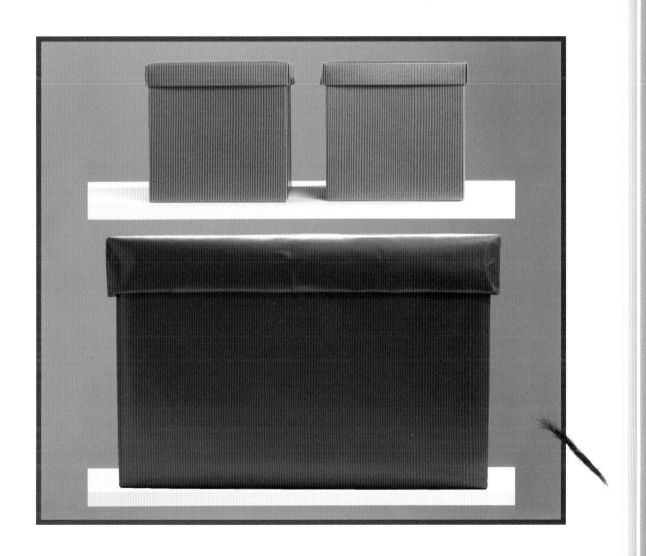

Two pink boxes can fit on the shelf.

Only one blue box can fit.

What does smaller mean?

These two chairs are the same size.

But the child is smaller than the man.

The child has more room when she sits in the chair.

Which is the smallest?

These dogs are named
Sport, Ginger, and Bitsy.

Bitsy is smaller than Ginger.

Sport is the smallest of all.

Can you tell which dog is Sport?

What does tiny mean?

This dog is very **small**.

He fits inside a little basket.

Something very small can also be called **tiny**.

This is a tiny dog.

What does too small mean?

These cookies have just been baked.

The cookies will not all fit in the cookie jar.

The cookie jar is too **small**.

What does bigger mean?

Bigger means there is more.

The girl's piece of pizza is bigger than the boy's.

Look at her **big** smile!

Which is the biggest?

The boy's balloon is bigger than either of the girls' balloons.

He has the biggest balloon.

It is a really **big** balloon.

It is so big that we could say
it is **huge**.

What does too big mean?

These children are playing "grown up".

They are dressed up in their parents' clothes.

The clothes are too **big**.

They laugh because they look
so funny!

What does size mean?

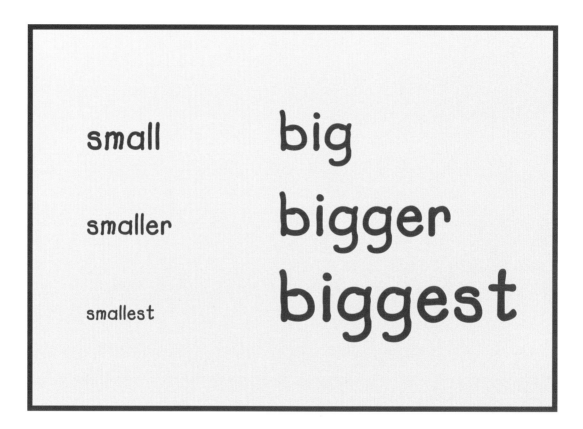

When we talk about **big** and **small**, we are talking about size.

There are some size words in the box.

little	large
teeny	huge
tiny	enormous

Here are more size words.

Quiz: True or False?

1. Size means how big or how small something is.

2. When something is tiny, it is very small.

3. A bus is bigger than a person.

4. When something is huge, it is very, very big.

Glossary

 **big** something that takes up a lot of room

 **huge** something that is very, very big

 **small** something that does not take up very much room

 **tiny** something that is very, very small

Index

Answers to quiz on page 22

1. True

2. True

3. True

4. True

Note to parents and teachers

Reading non-fiction texts for information is an important part of a child's literacy development. Readers can be encouraged to ask simple questions and then use the text to find the answers. Most chapters in this book begin with a question. Read the questions together. Look at the pictures. Talk about what the answer might be. Then read the text to find out if your predictions were correct. To develop readers' enquiry skills, encourage them to think of other questions they might ask about the topic. Discuss where you could find the answers. Assist children in using the contents page, picture glossary, and index to practise research skills and new vocabulary.